W9-AVX-159

Egypt
Classical Art Tours

Saqqara and Giza

Enrica Leospo

Translated by Eurolingua, Professional Language Services Ltd,
15-16 Newman Street, Oxford Street, London W 1P 3HD

Original title: Saqqara e Giza

Chief editors of ,,Classical Art Tours":
Silvio Locatelli und Marcello Boroli

© Manfred Pawlak Verlagsgesellschaft mbH, Herrsching
Distributed in the UK by Hawk Books Ltd

© Instituto Geografico de Agostini SpA, Novara

The "Throne of Eternity"

Saqqara and Giza. These two names immediately conjure up an image of ancient Egypt's best-known monuments – the pyramids – and especially the largest, the Cheops pyramid, with all the legends and speculation which have surrounded them since ancient times.

Having satisfied our first curious instincts, we find that there is an acceptable way to explain why these structures were created and what they mean. They are as meaningful as the ancient symbols they contain, and an easily deciphered witness to their age. Because of the almost total disappearance of written sources of information, it is archaeological finds that illustrate the beginnings of Egyptian history. The discoveries made about Saqqara during the III Dynasty (2680–2616 BC), have increased our understanding of an interesting cultural phase and, at the same time, reveal the outcome of a process of organisational and technological planning which had been underway for centuries. They also signal the promise of later development, the culmination of which is fully visible during the IV Dynasty (2615–2498 BC) in Giza. During this period, Egypt rationalised its own internal structure with surprising rapidity, by creating a well-constructed series of institutions, subsidiary to the main national government represented by the sovereign. The country's stability and well-being depended, firstly, on how land was used, subject to the river flooding, and also on the constant maintenance of the infrastructures responsible for agricultural productivity. The country's economy was influenced by these factors, which determined the quality of life and the very survival of the centralised state system. Because of his divine right, the king embodied all administrative, judicial, military and religious powers and the officials in charge of each department within this efficient system received their authority from him. The administrative decentralisation into *nomes* (provinces) was always kept under control by means of continuous correspondence with the capital and constantly updated reports of the situation in the suburban areas. These functions were carried out by scribes at both provincial and central government levels. One source of information about the State of the Old Kingdom was the lists of titles, some of which were purely honorary and therefore non-royal, engraved on the walls of the officials' tombs which were grouped around their kings' pyramids in ordered burial grounds. Through the formation of a ruling class assisting the sovereign, Egypt was therefore able to gain the resources necessary for radical technological progress during this particular period and, with the increasingly specialised division of labour, a social structure which provided a substantial workforce both for public buildings and for those representing pharaonic of divine power and authority.

As Egypt acquired a sense of history, political matters developed ideological and religious dimensions.

"Serve the king, O gods, because he is more ancient than the Great (the sun god) and has power on this throne". These words from the "Pyramid Texts" praise the concept of the divine nature of the sovereign worshipped like a god. The enormous power which royalty wielded also necessitated the formation of a basic monarchic system. On the one hand, this idea was inherent in the famous "Memphis theology" text, a late epigraphic copy of which has been discovered; on the other, it was manifest in the architecture and art which developed out of this political/religious context to serve both a commemorative and propagandist function. Egyptian art accurately mirrored the social structure of its time. While allowing itself some stylistic freedom in choice of subject, it began to establish certain functional standards for representing the ideology of continuity: the palace acquired continuity through the existence of a nearby temple.

All this was rapidly put into effect. The idea of stability and equilibrium achieved by a solid governmental body, perpetuate forever through the supernatural, was expressed in the vast, ostentatious monumental buildings and the use of stone for its "eternal" quality. Intelligent and diligent research then took this idea further by using purely rational, geometrical forms. The exaggerated size of the figures grew into more mature symbolism. From this point of view, therefore, the pyramid should not be seen simply as a royal tomb or funeral monument to perpetuate the memory of the sovereign but more as a specific expression of a vast cultural phenomenon.

The Monuments of the Djoser Complex

The finest example of this principle can be seen in Saqqara in the funerary complex of Djoser, a III Dynasty pharaoh. It is a monumental stone structure which rises up from the desert plateau above Memphis, the capital of the Old Kingdom. According to legend, Memphis was founded by Menes, the first Egyptian king who was half mythological and half historical. The tombs of ancient sover-

eigns (I–II Dynasties) were located there, but Djoser's architecture differs from these both in its typology and building techniques and in its meaning. In fact, the change from royal tomb to mastaba (that is, in the shape of a large parallelepipedon with tapering sides) in bare brick took on new semantic significance. Although it was the very beginning of the evolution of the pyramid, its transitional "step" phase was in itself (especially in this context) a consequence of more highly developed funerary concepts.

The architect who planned the complex was Imhotep, Djoser's Chancellor (equivalent to later positions such as Vizier or Prime Minister). He was later deified to commemorate his knowledge of all the arts and venerated in particular at a later date as the patron of the sciences and medicine, associated with Aesculapius by the Greeks. Stone architecture was unprecedented: it was Imhortep's invention and he used it to transform the old buildings of bare brick, wood and cane (materials which deteriorated quickly).

The complex, dominated by the "step" pyramid, was enclosed by a huge surrounding wall with bastions and recesses which resembled the White Wall of Memphis. A single entrance led into a columned corridor opening onto a wide court for the king's ritual procession during the jubilee festival (heb-sed). There was also a smaller lateral corridor dedicated to the jubilee rituals, flanked by chapels for the gods of Upper and Lower Egypt. A reminder of the split in the country can again be seen in two significant but not indistinct buildings which contain obvious references to the two territories: the "palaces" of the North and South. However, the actual function of the enclosure as a tomb is clear from other elements. Firstly, from the pyramid's funerary temple annexed to its northern side: the *serdab*, (the room for the deceased's statue) with the effigy of Djoser. Then there are the pyramid's ornate underground chambers which contained a magnificent collection of semi-precious stone and alabaster vases, proof of the artisans' expertise in working with such materials, as is also the reed-mat decoration on the walls in panels of blue glass tiles. Finally, there is the South Tomb, perhaps the second sepulchre, which continued the ancient tradition of building a double royal tomb – one for Lower Egypt in Saqqara and one for Upper Egypt in Abydos. The former was the real sepulchre, the latter a cenotaph. (A mastaba belonging to Djoser is also located in Beit Khallaf near Abydos.) The linking of the two tombs and their similar ritual edifices in one complex, built in immediate proximity to the capital of the unified country, accentuated the idea of a united kingdom guaranteed and reinforced by the sovereign of the time. The jubilee *(heb-sed)*, repeating the coronation ceremony, celebrated this reinforcement and renewal of regal power after a reign of thirty years. The gathering together of all the different funerary elements embodied in the *heb-sed* removed them from a fixed time and space. This tended to symbolise the continuity in the idea of the king's supernatural power which was independent of the physical, transitory person in which it was manifested.

Djoser's pyramid acquired its stepped appearance through various stages of planning. The original mastaba, later extended and increased in height to eventually become the base for further additions, was no longer sufficient to express the new political and religious concepts (Heliopolis sun worship prevailed) which the final staircase to the sky successfully evoked. There was another more concrete reason also: it could no longer be distinguished from the surrounding private sepulchres which were themselves becoming increasingly monumental.

Each component contributed to the expression of absolute values, and each single detail tended to create an abstract effect – the illusion of time and space – despite the functional implications of the buildings. In fact, one popular interpretation suggests that the collection of buildings within the funerary complex seems to copy those of Memphis: the king's palace, the administrative buildings of the two kingdoms and the sacella of the gods of Upper and Lower Egypt, continuing the tradition of the "tomb/dwelling place". However, the imitation is really only a model. The huge structures were mainly symbolic, consisting of niches for statues and short corridors for the performance of rituals, and there was no actual space inside. The buildings were made of great blocks of stone suitably arranged inside a sacred enclosure in accordance with ritual requirements.

The imitation in stone of materials used in the framework of lighter, ancient architecture contributes to the cementing or "freezing" in time of natural objects. For example, tree trunks became pillars; bundles of reeds became ribbed columns; reed-mat ceilings with their supports were faithfully reproduced in the decoration of stone ceiling blocks or the "rolled up" lintels forming a "tambour" above the doorways – quite apart from the other more obvious examples of capitals based on floral themes. We are presented with the successful attempt to turn a difficult thought process into a tangible object.

Djoser's architecture was continued, still in Saqqara, by his successor Sekhemkhet, whose recently discovered (1954) funerary monument was unfinished. His pyramid, a square layout, unlike Djoser's which was slightly rectangular, was also "stepped", with the same type of surrounding wall as his predecessor.

The Strictness of Size

The real change in royal funerary architecture took place during the IV Dynasty, coinciding with the changes in religious and political concepts. In the typological development we can see the gradual abandonment of the idea of the royal tomb as a manifestation of supernatural power, although it continued to remain the king's property. The open spaces for outdoor ritual celebrations amidst more mundane architectural settings were also abandoned in favour of a mythical concept of a sovereign who, after his death, was reborn as Osiris, whose mysteries were celebrated with funeral rites and various cult practices in more mystical surroundings demanding a long procession from the entrance to the sarcophagus chamber. It could be said that a somewhat secular vision of power became a religious vision.

For the first time, in Meidum, we find the combination of "valley building" – processional ramp – and "mortuary temple" annexed to the main pyramid, conforming with the new planimetry and themes. The pyramid was perhaps begun by Huni, the last III Dynasty pharaoh, but it was Seneferu, or rather his architect and eldest son Nefermaat, who devised the final plan. He obliterated its "staircase" formation and filled in the gap between the eight steps, a process which would be fully developed later.

There were two other pyramids attributed to Seneferu, as different from each other as they were from the first. The problems of planning and building a royal sepulchre are evident in these structures. They are loated in Dahshur, slightly south of Saqqara. The first chronologically, called the "rhomboidal" pyramid, it situated in the southern part of thes burial site and is one of the best preserved pyramid monuments. It is immediately recognisable from the two different gradients of its sides, giving it a unique profile. The most concrete and convincing explanation for this peculiarity is, that when the pyramid reached a certain height, the beginnings of a crack became apparent and the load borne by the structure had to be decreased in order to avoid the collapse of the vaults in the inner chambers. Symbolic reasons have also been given: there were two independent chambers with two separate entrances in the pyramid and the external appearance was meant to reflect this duplicity repeating the concept of the two linked tombs like those of Djoser. The other pyramid, the "northern" pyramid was called "Obtuse" because of its wide summit angle and the resulting moderate incline of its sides. It was also called the "pink" pyramid from the natural colour of the local stone used for its basic structure (the lighter limestone facing is missing) and it marks the last phase of pyramid building before the final uniformity established with the Cheops Pyramid. As the outer appearance altered, the internal structure also changed. The funerary chamber was no longer a hypogeum as in Djoser's pyramid, but partly dug out of the centre of the structure, while the layout of corridors and rooms was more linear and functional. Compared to Meidum, where the place of worship was limited to a funerary shrine with two steles and an altar, the other buildings in the complex were better designed, leaving more space for ritual worship.

The development of various aspects of these transitions can be recognised in different stages: building techniques, having benefited from experience, were no longer experimental but followed plans drawn up to ensure completion; the requirements of ritual religion were rigorously organised as soon as the building was finished and symbols expressed more clearly their intended message. The three pyramids of Giza are the most classic examples of this type of building and represent the best plan in the quest for monuments of vast dimensions which, beginning with Cheops, continued until the end of the Old Kingdom. The external proportions, a triangle with almost equilateral sides, together with the arrangement of the internal corridors and funeral chamber, were calculated with mathematical precision, with the base aligned exactly on the cardinal points. Only this scientific preparation and organised building, as well as the technical expertise in handling stone for the structures, can provide an explanation for such achievements. The technical/organisational complexities involved – cutting and transporting the stone from the quarry, structural plans, running the building site – are yet another confirmation of the presence of a stable government on which smoothly run programmes such as this could depend for extremely well-qualified and efficient technical and administrative guidance in the managing of large teams of labourers. Equally, the demand for better facilities for sacred worship within the layout of the fu-nerary complex was a sign of the clergy's increasing importance, destined to become antithetical to the pharaoh himself.

Cheops, Chephren and Mycerinus

The Cheops Pyramid (the architect was Hemiunu) has inspired a wealth of pseudo-scientific literature based on the esoteric significance of its dimensions and angles, and the calculations for its proportions. There are many contemporary stories written on this subject. To be more realistic, Hemiunu's plans simply included the best solutions to any experimental structural problems previously encountered – particularly that of how the gradient of the sides could ensure correct load distribution.

The inside of the pyramid was also built in a grander style. The final plan was changed, firstly to include a chamber called "the Queen's Chamber", in the middle of the pyramid on its central axis, and then another change, for which we do not know the exact reason, which was made to accommodate the sarcophagus chamber, above and slightly removed from the central axis and reached through a large gallery with impressive ceiling vaults plated with silver. Above the funeral chamber, five "relieving compartments", one on top of the other, with the top chamber ceiling made of appropriately "pointed" blocks, distribute the pressure caused by the weight of the structure. The quarry-marks with Cheops' name are visible on these granite blocks. The pyramid complex followed the design which had become common since Meidum, although the buildings have almost disappeared and the few remains of the causeways and the "valley building" have been encompassed by today's village.

The exceptional discovery in 1954 of two wooden boats (mainly made of pine) represent one of the main finds at the Cheops Pyramid. They had been dismantled into sections of and deposited in two cavities carved out to the rock along the south side of the pyramid. One of these has been totally restored and reconstructed and is kept in a museum close to where it was found. Other graves for sacred boats have been found near the same pyramid, to the side of the causeway or near other pyramids, and there is proof of their presence near royal mastabas during the first two dynasties. It is difficult to interpret the reason for the existence of these boats near the tombs. The significance could be "solar", alluding to the king's return from the sky in his boat as a sun god. "Sit in your place Unas, and navigate through the sky in your boat, O Ra;/the pole pushes your boat far from earth, O Ra;/here, you rise up at the horizon; and here, he holds your sceptre in his hand, like the navigator of your boat, O Ra", can be read in the "Pyramid Texts". The boat could also, however, have been connected with the funeral and the procession along the river to the burial site.

There was a very important discovery in 1925: that of the tomb of Queen Hetepheres, wife of Seneferu and mother of Cheops, whose funeral chamber was the only Old Kingdom royal tomb to be found intact, perhaps because it consisted of a well and funeral chamber with no superstructure. The original burial was probably at Dahshur, near the Seneferu Pyramid later desecrated and moved to this other site, near the first of the small "queen's" pyramids on the eastern side of the large pyramid. Many burial treasures, now in the Cairo Museum, were uncovered. Apart from the alabaster sarcophagus found empty, and a canopic vase and various receptacles made of the same material, a canopy, two chairs, a bed and a sedan-chair – all in gilded wood – were found, as well as beautifully crafted jewels such as silver anklets inlaid with malachite dragonflies, lapis lazuli and cornelians and some objets de toilette. The simple designs, carefully chosen materials and great technical expertise used to make these objects meant that they were extremely fine.

Compared to those already mentioned, the Chephren Pyramid was the first example of a burial site in which nearly all the elements of the established architectural "standards" were brought together in one whole. Although the details of the funerary temple next to the foot of the eastern side of the pyramid are now scarcely identifiable, its essentially functional structure can nevertheless be seen. There are two quite distinct sectors; one for the faithful, with an entrance hall and open courtyard; the other for worship, the actual sanctuary. Chephren's "valley building", connected to the entrance hall by a processional causeway, is the best-preserved example both of its kind and of all Old Kingdom monumental architecture. It was meant for ceremonies of purification and mummification and also incorporated the landing site for the river procession bearing the deceased's body. The main room, entered through a vestibule with two entrances, is a hypostyle hall in the form of an upside-down T. Its ceiling, made of granite ashlar tiles allowing rays of light to filter through narrow open slits, is supported by monolithic, granite pillars. The floor is covered with alabastrine limestone tiles. Twenty-three statues of the sovereign used to be placed against the walls. The pure, geometrical horizontal and vertical planes meeting in a right-angle were not decorated, but played on the use of materials and light for the intended aesthetic effect of monumentality in the building, to emphasise the richness of the stone and to create an effective impression of austerity. This was particularly noticeable when contrasted with the sacred rituals performed here. The impressive sphinx next to the temple further accentuates this effect, its composition visibly exemplifying the dogma of the sovereign's divinity, one of the cornerstones of the Heliopolis doctrine, and marking the greatest similarity between the god (the lion was a manifestation of the solar deity) and the king (the human head resembles Chephren and has typical royal features).

A different social structure developed at the end of the dynasty, with a distribution of wealth and authority which resulted in a balance of power hitherto focused on the pharaoh. This began with Mycerinus, and was reflected in less conspicuous funerary architecture which was typified by pyramids of smaller dimension, even though they were of the same style as earlier structures and enhanced up to a certain height with Aswan pink granite facing. It is obvious that less care was taken and building materials of inferior quality were used in some hurriedly finished parts of the complex. Other parts remained unfinished and were completed only later, in bare brick, by Mycerinus' son Shepseskaf in accordance with the original plan. This pharaoh was buried in Saqqara as opposed to Giza. Rather than a pyramid, his sepulchre was a colossal sarcophagus popularly called Mastabat el-Faraun. Similar in form to that of

his wife, Queen Khentkaues, in Giza it had walls incorporating large niches.

The fact that there are no tombs of dignitaries around the Mycerinus Pyramid is also significant. These were in vast cemeteries around other pyramids instead. At the end of the dynasty, the area was largely abandoned, although maintenance and restoration were carried out by the priests in charge of funeral rites, compensated for their continued service with endowments left to the temple by the king.

The "Pyramid Texts"

Whilst all this was happening, the private tomb began to be enlarged and embellished with splendid decoration, as can be seen in the V and VI Dynasty mastabas. This reveals the growth of a stratum of high officials to whom the king granted increasing privileges, in time leading to a relaxation of their subordination.

This pattern of development is equally apparent in the foundation of temples. In the V Dynasty (2497 – 2345 BC), the ancient, traditional Heliopolis creed provides many obvious examples. During this period, the old model of the temple consecrated to the cult of the sun god which rose in Heliopolis was adopted once more and centred on the impersonalised solar symbol of the obelisk, placed on a high podium in the middle of a large raised court incorporating an altar for outdoor worship. Of the mighty ruins of the sun temples, that of Niuserre in Abu Gurab, near of Abu Sir, is most easily identifiable, although others were situated nearby corresponding with burial sites built in the Abu Sir area by V Dynasty kings (Sahure, Neferirkare, Niuserre. Almost nothing remains of a fourth pyramid, that of Neferefre). These pyramids were less monumental in size, but the structure of the temples and annexed service buildings became more complex. Structures which took their form from nature prevailed: palmshaped columns in the courts, allusions to solar deities, internal wall decorations in the temples depicting cosmic concepts. Important papyri, of unique interest as a source of information about the royal cult, were found at Abu Sir.

Saqqara, where Userkaf, the first sovereign of the V Dynasty, had already built his pyramid, now becomes important once again. A fundamentally important new development in our understanding of religious changes during the Old Kingdom springs from the tomb of Unas, the last sovereign of the dynasty. The funeral texts, called the "Pyramid Texts", were engraved for the first time in the burial chamber of his pyramid and continued to be engraved for the entire duration of the VI Dynasty (2344–2180 BC) in the funeral chambers of kings from Teti to Pepi I, from Merenre to Pepi II as well as some queens. The most extensive are written in the vestibule and sarcophagus chamber of the Pepi II Pyramid. His funerary complex, together with that of Djoser, is the best preserved in the Saqqara area and was the basis for Maspero's publication and collation of the inscriptions into a collection now in the Berlin Academy. In 1881, this archaeologist made the sensational discovery of the Unas Pyramid.

Together with the development of funerary architecture, the "Pyramid Texts" document the continual change in concepts of extra-terrestrial life and related rituals. The spiritual arguments and political tensions of the period were set out on these wall-pages.

They consist of a sylloge of religious/funeral "formulae"with, although written as epigraphs at the end of the Old Kingdom, partly reflect old magical and mythical traditions (just as some graphic devices, had a magical purpose such as the the division in two of hieroglyphics depicting animated figures or only using a small number of symbols to avoid any harm to the deceased). Some of these formulae had been used in ancient times, while others were later drawn up specifically for temples. Because various types of texts were used in royal funeral rituals, their style is composite, incorporating hymns to the gods and royal cult rituals (including elements from coronations, mythological references, magic formulae and political and religious propaganda texts commemorating the demiurgic nature of the sovereign). "His mother, who inhabits the lower skies conceived him [the king],/his father Atum begot the king,/before the heavens existed,/before the earth existed,/before man had been created,/before the gods had been generated,/even before the existence of death."

The different origins and dates of this blended material are reflected in its contradictions and still more in the multiplicity of possible outcomes given as the supernatural destiny of the dead king. According to the oldest beliefs, he could become one of the circumpolar stars; he could alternatively be identified with the Sun, to whom Nut, the goddess of the sky, gave birth every day and then consumed every evening; or he could become the god Osiris.

The compilation of these texts must have taken place in Memphis because of the obvious tendency towards the Heliopolis creed, but they were rewritten and adapted to fit the cult's requirements, accepting and encompassing other religious beliefs the most popular of which was linked to the Osiris myth. It was not so much the search for a logical systemisation of the various beliefs, but a constant reaffirmation of certain basic concepts which once again played a part in the ideological conservatism of the ancient eastern world.

The Division of Labour

Taking Egyptian monumental architecture as a whole from the III Dynasty to the end of the Old Kingdom, we can say that one of its main characteristics was total exploitation of the technical and decorative qualities of stone, which was used with greater sophistication as more experience was gained. Ranging from the minute detail the small blocks of limestone used for Djoser's complex, to the megalithic masonry of Giza, these developments increase our understanding still more. Prior to the III Dynasty, stone was used in architecture only for some parts of the mastabas (architraves, door-jambs, façade tiles), while the main body of the edifice was made of bare brick, sometimes including wood or bamboo for the supporting structures. However, with Djoser, stone became a building material in its own right even though its full potential had not yet been realised.

Inferior quality local limestone was generally used for the basic structure, while a finer and more compact stone from Tura, Masara and other quarries located near the pyramids along the Nile's east bank was used for the external facing. The most valued types of stone – granite, basalt, diorite – came from the Aswan area, in Upper Egypt.

The location of the quarries shows how one of the main building problems was organising the transportation of the blocks of stone. As far as possible they were transported by barge along the river, using canals connecting with the Nile. Between the quarries and the river, they were transported on sledges or wooden sleds towed with ropes along the sand moistened to reduce friction, with the help of wooden rollers and levers. Traces of ports have been found near the "valley buildings" of the Giza pyramids. They were originally used as wharves during the construction of the pyramid and later became gathering places for those participating in the funeral ceremony and ritual procession which preceded the burial. The channels converging on the pyramid ports probably did not extend as far as the Nile, but joined a canal running parallel to it beginning in El Faiyum. Here it was fed by Lake Moeris and then flowed into Lake Mariut after reaching the river port of Memphis and crossing the western Delta. This canal permitted continual and regular work to be carried out, while the Nile was subject to flooding. An enormous ramp allowed material to be towed from the port to the pyramid building site. When work had been completed, the ramp was suitably adapted and elaborated to become a ceremonial road between the "valley building" and the pyramid temple. It was paved with limestone, with the two lateral walls decorated with bas-reliefs, and was sometimes covered.

While the ramp was being prepared, the area where the pyramid was to be built was levelled and its perimeter drawn out in a way which aligned with the cardinal points and allowed for its triangular shape. The alignment of its sides and corners was strictly controlled throughout the process, based on fixed reference points which served the purpose of compass. The blocks of stone were gradually transported onto the upper levels along bare brick "rolling" ramps, running closely parallel to the sides of the pyramid and set at a relatively low incline. Another great problem was co-ordinating the building to the horizontal blocks of the basic structure with that of internal chambers and corridors while constantly keeping in line with and checking the gradient. There was also the problem of when to position the "furniture" – the sarcophagus and the blocks of granite which were lowered inside to seal the entrance after the burial. Air ducts and "relieving compartments" also had to be built into the structure. Blocks for the façade and finishing touches were added, from the top downwards and the building ramps were gradually demolished from summit to base.

Unlike the compact mastabas built in horizontal layers, the pyramid at first appears to be a "girdle" structure, in other words, composed of a series of truncated pyramidal structures of decreasing height enclosing an internal truncated conical core. The "girdles" bare formed from blocks of stone leaning slightly inwards, each one smoothly polished to make it independent of the others and so giving greater flexibility to the structure as a whole. The gradations from one casing "girdle" to the next could then be filling in, in the same way as Meidum. During the IV Dynasty, a horizontal bed structure was used once more and, although inferior in quality, was much quicker to build. Building techniques changed fundamentally during the XII Dynasty in Dahshur and El Faiyum, favouring a structural frame and stone facing filled with brick which could be built faster and more cheaply, but was also less durable.

Work was organised into teams of labourers. Some were skilled (cutters, stone-dressers, polishers and decorators) and others were either permanent or part-time unskilled workers. There was also a maintenance team service on hand for the ramps and tools, supplies and provisions and a system of intermediaries who scheduled and controlled the work. Manual labour was not considered degrading but, as we mentioned before, was stimulated by a boom in the economy and a "reserve" of available workmen employed by the state and paid by the royal treasury with food, clothing and lodgings. (A fragment of a VI Dynasty papyrus, found in a sealed chamber in the Djoser Pyramid, records this in a letter protesting against an administration's inefficient system of payment). Interesting remains of labourers' quarters were found west of the Chephren Pyramid. Once the building work had been completed, these were given to the permanent employees – priests in charge of the funeral rites and labourers looking after the maintenance of monuments.

There is still a great deal of speculation about the building of pyramids, despite authoritative studies on the subject, like those of Rinaldi and Maragioglio. There are no Egyptian sources of information on building methods. Only mathematical papyri (like the Rhind Papyrus in the British Museum, London) demonstrate the Egyptians' skill in calculating volume and solving measuring problems. However, texts and illustrations relating to foundation ceremonies for sacred buildings do exist. These show how sites were fixed, how foundations were made and how materials were prepared and transported. (A relief of the Unas ramp depicts the columns for the king's funerary temple being transported by boat). Archaeological finds have included examples of measuring instruments and tools used to work the stone.

The Mastabas

While the enormous pyramid complexes were under construction, vast cemeteries of mastabas for members of the royal family, dignitaries and state officials were built around them.

The term used for this type of structure, mastaba, is of Arabic origin. They were originally royal tombs but adopted by private citizens from the III Dynasty onwards. As already mentioned, the structure was a large parallelepipedon with tapered sides, made of bare bricks until the III Dynasty, but then later also of stone. A space was reserved in the superstructure for a ramp or shaft descending into the burial chamber. The place of worship, which took various forms, initially consisted of a shrine or niche, traditionally called the "false door", to the east of the main part of the structure, with steles and a table for offerings. Other small rooms for worship were added later and gradually extended. At first, the superstructure was solid, made totally of brick with walls sometimes moulded. The layout of the mastaba became more open and, with the VI Dynasty, at the culmination of its typological development, the inside was adapted into a series of chambers the walls of which were decorated with a cycle of drawings following a carefully thought out plan. The reliefs were executed with the latest techniques. Sometimes niches for high relief

statues were carved into the walls, or the *serdab* hid a full statue of the deceased. In the early IV Dynasty mastabas, the presence of the "reserve head" deposited in the bottom of the shaft was a typical feature. As we have seen in royal architecture, statues, an essential feature of burials, served as substitutes and were not simply commemorative as their location in tombs and temples might suggest. They were a projection of the person who, through them, continued to live. As well as magnificent examples of stone and wooden sculpture, numerous painted limestone statuettes have been discovered in the mastabas. These, like the wall decorations painted for the same reason, are also linked to the concept of survival.

All the subjects represented relate to the owner of the tomb and his position in society. Their purpose is not simply to illustrate ritual offerings or events of his funeral, but to guarantee his eternal life. At first (in the III Dynasty and the beginning of the IV Dynasty), decoration was limited to the funerary shrine which was decorated with a scene of the offering being made to the deceased. It was then extended to the chapel walls, featuring rows of male and female figures bearing offerings, sacrificial animals and scenes connected with the ritual. The theme was later elaborated and the inner chambers to accommodate these paintings. Events from daily life such as hunting and fishing, raising cattle, farming, the preparation of food (bread, beer, meat), crafts (metal, stone, wood and other materials, the production of vases and other receptacles, spinning and weaving) are depicted here, and other less common themes can be seen elsewhere. The various scenes were carefully laid out to fit the place of worship, where continued offerings were made possible by the royal deceased's endowment.

There was no reference to the private life. He appears only as a public figure in the context of his social status with references to his name, honorary titles and position.

The principles governing ancient eastern life, which placed greater emphasis on the values of society as a whole rather than those of the individual, had a parallel in the development of artistic principles. The work of an individual artist depended on certain accepted and clearly formulated methods such as the reduction of the figure to a geometric design. Architectural space and figurative design were also based on certain criteria and governed by this same "conceptual realism".

The different stages of development in monumental Egyptian architecture can be seen in the remains of other areas: initially, in the provinces of Middle and Upper Egypt where the local governors had, in the course of decentralising state administration, acquired great autonomy; and then later mainly in Thebes, the capital of the new Kingdom.

However, the areas of Saqqara and Giza continued to maintain their importance and the Hellenic and Roman ages were to leave significant historical and archaeological evidence.

As soon as they were built, the monuments were desecrated and devastated, and many completely destroyed. However, their fame has survived all the ages of literary and figurative art. In Egyptian literature, the pyramids of the ancient kings had already become legendary, and the legends surrounding them have fascinated travellers and writers since the time of the ancient classics. Herodotus embroidered historical accounts of the period with anecdotes and stories of his trip to Egypt.

Arabic folklore filled the pyramids with ghosts and buried treasure. The accounts of pilgrims to the Holy Land relate the oldest legend of all; they saw the pyramids as Joseph's granaries (and they are depicted as such in St Mark's, Venice). The popularity of the pyramids can be gauged from the exoteric explanations of modern "pyramidology", covering every aspect of the argument from the most curious to the most absurd, but systematic scientific research should no doubt be able to overcome all these theories.

Figures of bearers in the chapel of the Ti Mastaba in Saqqara; the detail is part of a farming scene.

The Burial Sites of Saqqara

The archaeological site of Saqqara, extending about eight kilometres, includes various burial sites. The largest of these is the Djoser complex, with the "step" pyramid and funerary monuments as the focal point. On the two preceding pages is a view of the pyramid itself from the courtyard of the *hep-sed* (jubilee), to the south-east, surrounded by votive chapels. The oldest part of the Saqqara site, to the north, includes royal tombs with bare brick superstructures from the I Dynasty and various II Dynasty graves. The importance of this area in the III Dynasty diminished during the period which followed, when Giza became more prominent. With Unas (end of the V Dynasty), the building of royal pyramids and elaborate mastabas was systematically undertaken once more, resulting in the monumental features which still distinguish them today. There were no more significant additions until the New Kingdom (1570 – 1070 BC), although the cult of the old sovereigns continued. In the XVIII Dynasty, Saqqara again extended the tombs of high state officials. The Tomb of General Haremhab, with its splendid bas-reliefs, is most noteworthy. Saqqara's continued importance is reflected in the restoration and reconstruction of numerous old monuments during the XIX Dynasty. During the period which followed, interest in preserving the royal burial sites waned and some of the temples were in fact used for storing building materials. During this period the cemetery of the Hapi sacred bulls, known by its Greek name Serapeo, was extended (having originated in the XVIII Dynasty). It was a complex of underground galleries containing rows of the animals' impressive granite sarcophagi. This burial ground became the site of privileged worship. During the XXX Dynasty, and later under the Ptolemys, it was changed into a complex of monuments where religious and funerary edifices stood next to administrative buildings (priests' houses, schools, hostels, a market, a sanatorium). Accounts dating from the Hellenic-Roman age, are supplemented by others from the Coptic era which, with the convent of St Jeremiah (founded in 430 AD during the second half of the tenth century), provide a conclusion to the history of the site's development.

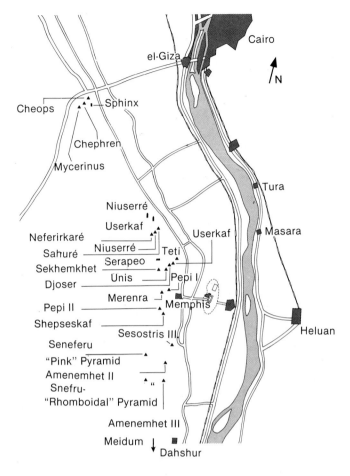

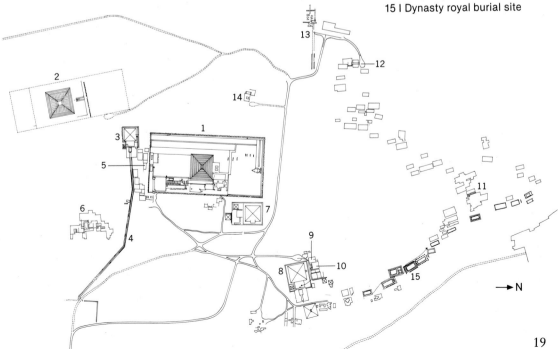

Left: map of the sites of the main pyramids built between the III and XII Dynasties between Cairo and Dahshur. Meidum, the site of the Seneferu Pyramid, is further south. Along the right bank of the Nile are the main quarries used at that time for good quality limestone. Below: map of the archaeological area of Saqqara:

1 The Djoser funerary complex
2 The Sekhemkhet funerary complex
3 Unas Pyramid
4 Approach ramp to the Unas Pyramid
5 Idut Mastaba
6 Convent of St Jeremiah
7 Userkaf Pyramid
8 Teti Pyramid
9 Mereruka Mastaba
10 Kagemni Mastaba
11 Tomb of Hesira
12 Ti Mastaba
13 Serapeo
14 Ptahhotep Mastaba
15 I Dynasty royal burial site

The serdab (below) can be seen next to the Djoser Pyramid, on the north side. It is a small chamber, sealed on all sides, which contained the statue of the deceased who communicated with the outside world through holes in the wall at eye-level. The painted limestone statue of Djoser (right) was found here and is now in the Egyptian Museum, Cairo. The figure is wrapped in the cloak worn by the king during the heb-sed or jubilee ceremonies. On his head he wears the nemes, a pleated fabric headdress. He is also wearing a false beard.

Left, a photograph showing the entrance colonnade to the sacred enclosure of the Djoser Pyramid. It consists of two rows of twenty engraved ribbed columns beyond which lies the wide court. On the southern side of this court is the South Tomb, thought to be the second of the royal sepulchres or perhaps the room meant for the canopic vases containing the entrails removed from the body for mummification. As in the pyramid, the numerous underground chambers here were tiled with blue faïence. In one of the rooms there are three bas-reliefs depicting the king performing rituals like the heb-sed (far left, top; photograph: Egyptian Museum, Turin). The relief's frame bears the royal titles, surrounded by blue faïence tiles in the reed-mat pattern with the cylindrical tambour above the relief representing a rolled up mat. The funerary apartment is thought to be a symbolic reproduction of the royal palace. Far left, bottom: the moulded wall, with a frieze of cobras, forming the east façade of the South Tomb sanctuary.

The wall surrounding the Djoser complex is about 1.50km long and originally more than 10m high, with moulded ramparts imitating a fortified wall. There is only one entrance, but fourteen false doors have been carved into the recesses at various intervals. From the southern side of the wall (left, top) there is a view of the Unas Pyramid, now almost completely in ruins (left, bottom). The "Pyramid Texts" were engraved for the first time in its inner funeral chamber (below: photograph Tosi-Lovera).

To the east of the Unas
Pyramid, one can walk along
the remains of the processional
causeway which led from the
"valley building" to the "high
temple". It is more than 700m
long and 2.60m wide and
formed a type of gallery paved
in limestone and flanked by
two Tura limestone walls – of
which a great deal remains –
with a ceiling decorated with
stars but pierced with slits
which allowed the light to filter
through. The internal walls
were originally decorated with
bas-reliefs and the few which
remain, of great artistic value,
show a curious descriptive
liveliness, as in the market
scene which shows produce
being exchanged, fishmongers
and a wandering minstrel
with his monkeys. The realism
in the description of themes
such as famine, with its skeletal
human figures, is unusually
stark. To the immediate south
of the causeway are two large
boat-shaped graves dug out of
the rock side by side and about
40m long and lined with fine
quality limestone (below).
These were used for the boats,
or their simulacrums, which
were always buried near the
sepulchre, although the exact
meaning of the tradition is
uncertain.

During the excavations along the external wall of the Djoser enclosure, the Mastaba of Princess Idut was discovered. She was probably Unas' daughter and lived between the end of the V and beginning of the VI Dynasties. The tomb, built for a vizier, was appropriated for her. The chapel with the funerary shrine is located in the very middle of the superstructure and can be entered by passing through rooms decorated with fine reliefs with fishing, hippopotamus hunting and funeral scenes (the transportation of the statue of the tomb). The last two chambers, the chapel and its antechamber (left) were dedicated to the presentation of offerings, the element most closely linked to the funeral ritual and represented by the images on the walls. These scenes show rows of figures bearing offerings and animals being slaughtered for sacrifice. Opposite, top: two men with flint knives can be seen cutting up an ox. Bottom: the removal of the right front leg, one of the offerings most prized. All around there are assistants sharpening knives and holding the animals still. Illustrated texts accompany the reliefs.

The Mastaba of Ti is one of the largest and most ornate in the Saqqara site. Its main features are a wide court with twelve pillars which was used for sacrifices or family gatherings, and the chapel, where one can look through three slits and see the statue of Ti in the serdab. It was a family tomb which also included the sepulchres of his wife and one son. Ti, who lived during the first half of the V Dynasty, was an inspector of the Neferirkare and Niuserre pyramids and sun temples at Abu Sir and superintendent of the prophets. On the preceding pages are some typical examples of mastaba decoration. Left, top: detail of a scene showing food being prepared, with scribes recording the deliveries made (the relief is located in the chamber intended for bread, jugs of beer, wine and other supplies). Bottom: an episode from one of the chapel walls. A herd of oxen returning from pasture is seen crossing a branch of the Nile Delta. On the facing page: again in the chapel, farmers from Ti's property return carrying the agricultural produce, birds and other animals.

In the Chapel of the Ti Mastaba, at the centre of the north wall, is a scene showing hippopotami being hunted in a swamp, amongst a clump of reeds, of which the stalks form the background of the scene (on these two pages). Four men with harpoons and ropes standing in a light boat also made of reeds are in the process of capturing the animals which were numerous in the Nile in those days. One of the hippopotami clenches in his jaws a crocodile struggling to escape. The detail comes from a series depicting one of Ti's boat trips across the Delta. Hippopotamus hunting was one of the most common themes in these scenes of daily life. It later became a ritual motif, symbolising the killing by a benevolent god (almost always Horus) of the ferocious beast, itself identified with an evil god. The accuracy of each detail and the realistic description of everyday events in and around the Nile are worth noting for the knowledge and experience of the area, its terrain and animals which can be passed on to us.

33

The reliefs shown on these pages were carved in the Mastaba of
Ptahhotep and his son Akhethotep, "inspectors of the pyramid
priests" of Abu Sir (V Dynasty), and are part of larger scenes
depicting animals for offerings. One should note the rhythmic
composition of the ordered rows of birds, divided into species —
cranes, geese, ducks, pigeons — repetitive and yet full of
movement. Right: a herdsman leading a huge ox with lyre-shaped
horns is assisted by a companion pushing the animal.

Left: a relief in the Mastaba of Ptahhotep. The deceased, seated before the offerings table and wearing the panther skin of a priest, extends his right hand towards the table to accept the offering granted to him by royal concession. With his left hand, he raises a glass to his lips. The offerings are depicted in rows, laid one above the other, in accordance with the typical Egyptian orthogonal image of perspective. Right: a photograph of the Mastaba of the vizier Mereruke – one of the largest in Saqqara – showing the chapel with the niche containing the statue of the deceased. "Director of All the King's Works" and "Palace Administrator" during the reign of Teti (VI Dynasty). On the following pages is a relief from the same mastaba, with scenes of goldsmiths at work. Top, various stages of the metalwork are shown: smelting (the workers are blowing through tubes to poke the fire), pouring and hammering. Bottom, the manufacture of various types of necklaces by dwarf workers, with the finished objects and the registers of the furnaces also shown.

Two views of the Mastaba of Kagemni, Vizier and Minister of Justice during the VI Dynasty. Opposite: the chapel with the funerary shrine, altar and a small flight of steps leading to it. On this page: the series of rooms preceding the chapel itself. The pages which follow show (left) a photograph of a wooden panel, now in the Egyptian Museum in Cario, originating from the Tomb of Hesy-Re, a high official during the III Dynasty. The deceased is seated at the table of offerings. Scribes' tools hang from his right shoulder and his left hand holds a cane and sceptre. Right: the wooden funerary shrine of Ika and his wife Imerit, priestess of Hathor (IV Dynasty), in the Cairo Museum. This follows a typical layout, composed of a tablet – with tambour at the top: showing the deceased, or in this case two deceased people, at the funeral table, and an architrave and jambs with hieroglyphic inscriptions including the owners' names and titles, pictures of them and the formula for the offering.

Left: a large funerary shrine (3.40m high and 2.20m wide) from the Mastaba of Iteti, "Chief of the Ten of Upper Egypt" and "Inspector of Transport" who lived between the end of the V and beginning of the IV Dynasties (Cairo Museum). A high relief statue of the owner is carved in the central niche. The shrine is designed according to the conventional plan, with the tablet decoration showing the deceased before the offerings table. The list of offerings is written in hieroglyphics on the side panels with another figure of the deceased on both bases.

Above: a beautiful alabaster offerings table (Cairo, Egyptian Museum) of Seneferu-nefer, from the VI Dynasty (50cm wide). On this one can see the enlarged hieroglyphic sign hetep *(offering), surrounded by cavities for liquids. In the bottom left corner, inside a circle representing bread, is a detailed description of the offerings granted by the king to ensure the deceased's eternal life. In accordance with the accepted formula for offerings, they are listed in quantities of a thousand: one thousand loaves of bread, one thousand jugs of beer, one thousand oxen, birds, alabaster vases and garments.*

The photographs on the preceding pages show two beautiful statues of prisoners (Cairo Museum). The face (detail, preceding right page) is characterised by features attributing the figures to an ethnic group from the Near East. These, and numerous other sculptures of prisoners found in pieces, were probably positioned along the causeways of the Pepi I Pyramid (VI Dynasty) to represent the nations over which the sovereign ruled.

Right: the precious sycamore statue of Ka-aper, the "first lector priest" who lived during the V Dynasty (Cairo Museum). The 1.10m tall figure is made from one piece of wood, except for the arms which are attached by wooden pins. The inset eyes are of a different material. The figure is in a full frontal position with his left leg in front of his right, and right arm hanging by his side. His right hand once grasped a sceptre (now lost) and his left arm is bent to hold a stick. His clothing, consisting of a simple skirt knotted at the waist, and the objects which Ka-aper is holding, are elements typical of private statuary. The face is extremely realistic.

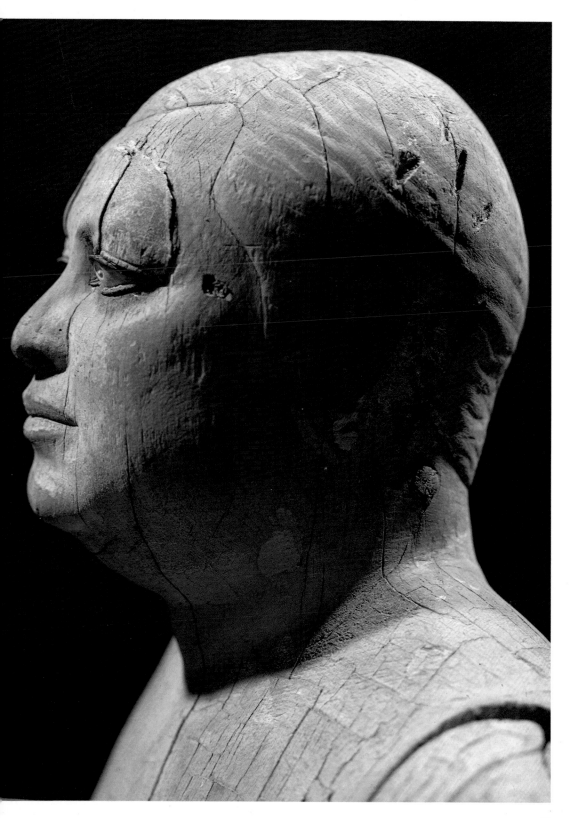

The pyramids of Meidum and Dahshur mark the transitional phase between the "step" pyramid and the well-defined geometric pyramid. The present appearance of the Seneferu Pyramid (top, photograph Lovera), like a "tower", has been caused by later dismantling which uncovered five of the different levels formed by the "girdles" surrounding the core. The funeral chamber is reached through a corridor descending from the entrance in the north face, 20m above the ground (bottom, photograph Tosi-Lovera). This chamber was partly dug out of the rock and partly dug out of, as it were, the core of the superstructure, with a typical false vaulted ceiling created by overhanging blocks of stone. Inscriptions left by New Kingdom visitors in the funerary temple confirm that the pyramid was completed for Seneferu. The blocks of stone in the pyramid at Meidum bear the same quarry-marks as the "rhomboidal" pyramid in Dahshur which was definitely built for this sovereign and the surrounding tombs all belonged to Seneferu's officials.

In Dahshur, the "rhomboidal" pyramid with the double gradient, built in the southern part of the site (top), has been attributed to Seneferu because his name was found on two stone blocks inside. The two funeral chambers, entered through two separate entrances, one in the north face and the other in the west, also have false vaults. The first was dug completely out of the rock, the other from the centre of the pyramid. This pyramid was abandoned for structural reasons, and a second pyramid was built (centre, photograph Egyptian Museum, Turin). This is called "obtuse" because of the gentler gradient of its sides. It is also called "pink" because of the colour of the local limestone and lacks the final white Tura limestone facing. Inside, in the solid rock base, are three chambers with false vaults, but there are no traces of royal sepulchres. Bottom: a view of Abu Sir where V Dynasty pyramids and sun temples were located – probably based on the design of the great temple of Heliopolis. In the background, one can see the Pyramid of Sahure, and in the foreground the remains of the "valley building".

The Archaeological Site of Giza

Recent excavations at the archaeological site of Giza, established during the IV Dynasty, have revealed the existence of an even older settlement (of dwellings and tombs) dating to the Tanite age (first two dynasties). However, the area's most outstanding features are the group of three pyramids of Cheops, Chephren and Mycerinus with the mortuary temples linked to them (right), the sphinx, and the mastabas arranged in regular parallel lines. This system was later changed by the addition of new structures which disturbed the original layout. These began with the tombs of V and VI Dynasty civil servants and religious officials, followed later by those of leading figures from the Saite age (XXVI Dynasty) and the Persian (XXVII Dynasty) who considered it a privilege to have their tombs near the great pyramids. Below, a map of Giza: 1 Cheops Pyramid. 2 Chephren Pyramid. 3 Mycerinus Pyramid. 4 Satellite pyramids. 5 Cheops boats. 6 Chephren's "valley building". 7 Sphinx. 8 Mastabas. 9 Tomb of Hetepheres. 10 Tomb of Khentkaues.

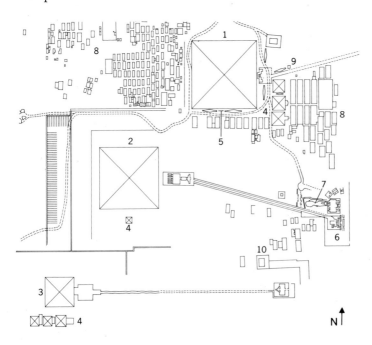

The size and quality of the Cheops Pyramid (opposite, top) represents the zenith of pyramid building. It is now 137m high (originally 146), and the angle of the gradient of its sides is 51 degrees, which provided the best solution for structural purposes. Although it is apparently in tact, its external casing was in fact removed (taken by the Arabs to be used as building material) together with twelve layers of stone blocks at the summit or piramidion (the point).
Opposite, bottom: The Chephren Pyramid, lower (143 m originally, reduced to 136) but on a raised site so that today it seems taller. It retains its limestone facing at the top, looking like some kind of hood and some blocks of pink granite can still be found at the base. The beautiful diorite statue, now in the Cairo Museum (left), comes from a well in the Chephren "valley building" and portrays the sovereign on his throne. A falcon (the god Horus) behind his head protects him with its widespread wings. The throne of the statue, which represents the king's divinity, bears the symbol of Upper and Lower Egypt on its side.

A complex of mastabas for high officials also developed near the Chephren Pyramid (as in the cemeteries to the east and west of the Cheops Pyramid). They were neatly arranged in fairly close parallel rows. Some scholars believe this layout to be an early form of town-planning. The mastabas have a superstructure in solid stone, with a convex roof. The foreground of the photograph shows a section of this burial site with some of these tombs. The Chephren Pyramid can be seen in the background.

The "valley building" of Chephren was built partly of granite and partly of limestone dressed with granite tiles. The external walls are built at a slight angle (seen as a whole, it must have looked like a monumental mastaba, particularly from the point of view of the façade.) Inside, the hypostyle hall (below) consists of sixteen monolithic pink granite pillars and alabaster paving contrasting with the black granite walls to create a very strikingly colourful effect. The ceiling was composed of long granite blocks supported by pillars.

The Chephren Pyramid is not aligned with its "valley building" because, to avoid subsidence, a rocky bridge which crossed over the sinking ground to obliquely reach the plateau was used as the foundation for the causeway. On the north side of this building, a corridor (photograph, left) led to the entrance to the pyramid. Once outside, one immediately sees the sphinx on the right, with the temple dedicated to it and the pyramid itself in the background (see over). The sphinx was built from a boulder found in the limestone quarries north of the "valley building". It has a lion's body and human head resembling Chephren, with the usual royal features, and was finished with coloured stucco. A temple with a central court and lateral halls (right) made of enormous blocks of limestone and probably dressed with granite was erected in front of the sphinx. It was not a funerary temple, but was built for divine worship or perhaps for coronation ceremonies. The two temples together create one uniform whole.

Left: a close-up of the sphinx showing its majestic proportions (20m tall and 57m long). Between the paws one can see the curved top of Tuthmosis IV's "stele of dreams", which tells how the pharaoh, after lying in the sphinx's shadow and dreaming that the sun god appeared to him complaining of neglect, ordered the unearthing and restoration of the monument. Below: detail of a statue of Mycerinus (Cairo Museum) from his "valley building".

Top: the Mycerinus Pyramid, approximately 63m high, viewed from the south with the three small "satellite" pyramids. These structures were often found next to royal pyramids and were also almost always funeral buildings, such as tombs of queen mothers or princesses of royal blood. They were much smaller but took the same form as the large pyramids with the inner funeral chambers and places of worship reduced to bare essentials. The funeral chambers inside contained granite sarcophagi. Bottom: the north face of the Mycerinus Pyramid with the obvious breach made by the Mamelukes when trying to find the entrance. In the final plan of the funeral apartment, a descending gallery led to the sarcophagus chamber, dressed in granite, with a false vaulted ceiling. The magnificent basalt sarcophagus was lost in a shipwreck while being transported to England. The Mycerinus Pyramid is called the "painted pyramid" in Arabic, perhaps because it was originally covered with a layer of stucco or mortar.

Only part of the mortuary temple of Mycerinus (left page overleaf), situated next to the east side of the pyramid, was built during his reign. It was completed, like the rest of the complex, by his successor Shepseskaf, although with a plastered bare brick casing and not entirely in stone. It is clear from the plan of this temple that there were two quite distinct areas for different uses. One part, incorporating a large, internal, pillared courtyard, was accessible and used for daily services to the deceased king. The other part, comprising an altar for offerings and steles, was sealed off and directly connected to the pyramid. The Mycerinus Pyramid was a fine facing of 16 rows of pink Aswan granite blocks (right) all the way round the base. The blocks are not all polished, which shows that finishing touches such as these took place after the blocks were in position, so as to prevent any breaches at the corners caused by moving them. The top part of the pyramid was dressed with white Tura limestone.

The tombs of Qar and Idu are situated in the northernmost part of the great eastern burial site of the Cheops Pyramid. The two mastabas are anomalous because their superstructure, scarcely visible now, seemed to consist of an enclosed area with a chapel of rock made accessible via a staircase. Qar was an administrator of the property around the Pyramid of Pepi I (VI Dynasty) and "palace superintendent". (It is not clear whether he was Idu's father or vice versa.) The pillared chamber (opposite) preceding the offerings chamber contains a line of high-relief statues all inside one niche along the south wall. They were meant to both protect and take the place of the deceased, so ensuring his eternal life. The Mastaba of Idu, to the east of the other, contains an equally large quantity of sculpture. In the offering chamber (right), dug out of the rock, are six statues in separate niches with the names and titles of the deceased inscribed on the architraves and jambs: they include "scribe of royal letters" and "chief of the servants' scribes" assigned to temple property.

69

A funerary shrine (below) can be seen in the offering chamber of the Mastaba of Idu and is typical apart from the lower section which was recarved into a niche containing an unusual figure of the deceased: a bust, with hands extended towards the offerings table in front of him. Right: detail of the shrine, showing the tablet picture of Idu sitting before the table. The miniature figure of his wife, Meretites, is under his chair. The columns of hieroglyphics above the table describe the various types of objects belonging to the deceased.

These two pages illustrate some of the finds from other tombs in Giza. The two statues of scribes (Cairo Museum) from the IV Dynasty are seated cross-legged in the typical position, the tablet, on which the papyrus was placed for writing, on their knees. The scribe on the left bows his head slightly forwards to look at the page. The figure below is staring straight ahead, in keeping with the strictest rules of frontal representation. Both statuettes are in brightly painted limestone.

Below: detail of a painted limestone statue (V Dynasty) originally from Giza and now in the Cairo Museum. The statue opposite, of a woman preparing beer (V Dynasty) is also from Giza (Cairo Museum). Figures of workers or craftsmen employed in the preparation of food and drink were common in Old Kingdom tombs. They were connected with magical/religious concepts of the deceased's eternal life and the principle that demanded offerings and wall decorations was also responsible for their presence in the tombs.

Index